PILGRIMAGE REFLECTIONS

Journal

CREATED FOR YOU BY

TANIA MAREE HERBERT

BALBOA.PRESS

A DIVISION OF HAY HOUSE

Balboa Press books may be ordered through booksellers or by contacting:

Balboa Press
A Division of Hay House
1663 Liberty Drive
Bloomington, IN 47403
www.balboapress.com.au
AU TFN: 1 800 844 925 (Toll Free inside Australia)
AU Local: 0283 107 086 (+61 2 8310 7086 from outside Australia)

Print information available on the last page.

ISBN: 978-1-5043-0675-1 (sc)
ISBN: 978-1-5043-0676-8 (e)

Balboa Press rev. date: 07/16/2020

This journal belongs to

_____

Date

_____

Name of Pilgrimage

_____

Dedication

This journal is dedicated to my two Camino angels,
and to you also, dear Pilgrim.
Buen Camino!

Introduction

I created this journal for you as a special place for you to record your pilgrimage experiences.

Pilgrimage presents you with a gift of time for personal reflection. I encourage you to ponder and write down the things that touch or speak to your heart.

Personally, I have found it to be a relaxing practice at the end of each day to reflect upon the day's events—the sights, sounds, conversations, and happenings—and to jot down my thoughts or feelings about them. Sometimes I simply wrote down the names of the places I visited that day, the name of a meal that I enjoyed, or something that someone said that made me smile. On other occasions, I found inspiration or became aware of something to be grateful for. It is with gratitude that I share with you the fact that the seed for creating this journal was born from my pilgrimages to Santiago de Compostela.

On return to your home, the following pages will hold for you precious memories to share with others or to keep for your own personal reflection.

As you embark on your journey, I wish you safe travels, insightful experiences, and many moments of joy and wonder.

Wishing you well,
Tania

INSPIRATION

What inspired this journey?

Before you leave for your pilgrimage take a few moments to reflect upon

◊   what has led you to embark on this Pilgrimage;
◊   who or what has inspired you;
◊   interesting facts about the destination(s) you are travelling to;
◊   what are you most looking forward to;
◊   what do you hope to receive from this experience?

Inspiration for this journey…

Inspiration for this journey…

REFLECTIONS

Pilgrim Shells
2019 Photograph courtesy of Germán Limeres

Your Pilgrimage

On the following pages, there is space for you to record your pilgrimage reflections.

As a guide, during or at the end of each day, recall

◊   what you saw, heard, tasted, smelt, or touched;
◊   conversations you had with others;
◊   signs or symbols you noticed;
◊   something that may have inspired you or made you feel grateful; or
◊   thoughts or feelings you had.

Write down the things that resonated with you.
You may even wish to draw on these pages.
This is a sacred space for your memories and reflections.
Enjoy!

Day _____ Date _____

Day _____ Date _____

My reflections ...

Day _____ Date _____

Day _____ Date _____

My reflections ...

Day _____ Date _____

My reflections …

Day _____ Date _____

My reflections ...

HOPE

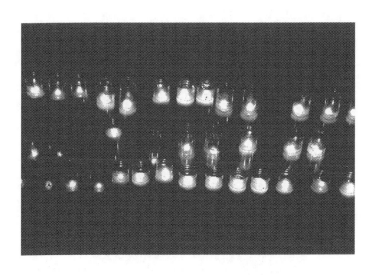

Candles – Light of Hope
2019 Photograph courtesy of Germán Limeres,

Day _____ Date _____

My reflections …

Day _____ Date _____

My reflections ...

Day _____ Date _____

My reflections ...

Day _____ Date _____

My reflections ...

Day _____ Date _____

My reflections ...

Day _____ Date _____

My reflections ...

Day _____ Date _____

My reflections ...

COMPANIONS

Kenzo – on the Way to Portamarin
2015 Photograph courtesy of Germán Limeres

Day _____ Date _____

Day _____ Date _____

My reflections …

Day _____ Date _____

My reflections ...

Day _____ Date _____

Day _____ Date _____

Day _____ Date _____

My reflections …

TRUST

Follow the Arrow
2019 Photograph courtesy of Germán Limeres

Day _____ Date _____

Day _____ Date _____

My reflections ...

Day _____ Date _____

My reflections …

Day _____ Date _____

Day _____ Date _____

My reflections …

Day _____ Date _____

My reflections …

Day _____ Date _____

PRAY

The Rosary
2019 Photograph courtesy of Germán Limeres

Day _____ Date _____

Day _____ Date _____

Day _____ Date _____

Day _____ Date _____

My reflections …

Day _____ Date _____

My reflections ...

Day _____ Date _____

My reflections ...

Day _____ Date _____

FAITH

Devotion – Jesus I Place My Trust in You
2016 Photograph by Tania Maree Herbert

Day _____ Date _____

Day _____ Date _____

Day _____ Date _____

Day _____ Date _____

Day _____ Date _____

My reflections …

Day _____ Date _____

My reflections …

Day _____ Date _____

My reflections …

Day _____ Date _____

My reflections …

KINDNESS

Be an Angel along the Way
2016 Photograph by Tania Maree Herbert

Day _____ Date _____

My reflections …

Day _____ Date _____

Day _____ Date _____

Day _____ Date _____

My reflections …

Day _____ Date _____

STRENGTH

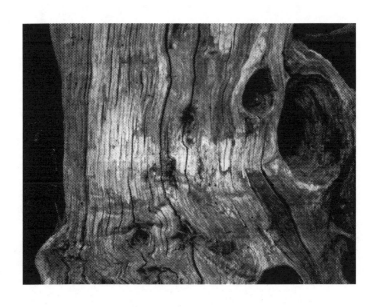

At the Heart of Nature
2018 Photograph courtesy of Germán Limeres

Day _____ Date _____

My reflections …

Day _____ Date _____

Day _____ Date _____

My reflections ...

Day _____ Date _____

My reflections …

Day _____ Date _____

Day _____ Date _____

Day _____ Date _____

JOY

Finding the Way
2019 Photograph courtesy of Germán Limeres

The following pages provide you with space for notes, reminders, drawings, contact details of people that you met on your pilgrimage, ideas, or future plans.

Notes ...

Notes ...

Notes …

Notes ...

Notes …

LOVE

Love – In the Simple Things in Life
2019 Photograph by Tania Maree Herbert

Your return home

This space is available to you to write down any further thoughts that you may have on returning home or in the future, as you flick through the pages of this journal and recall your pilgrimage.

Notes …

Notes …

Acknowledgements

To Saint James of the Camino de Santiago de Compostela – your example of Faith, embodied in the qualities of attentive listening, humility and perseverance are inspirational.

To my family, cousins, friends, colleagues, guides, and my two "Camino families" who have enriched my pilgrimages, holiday, and work travels over the years—your footprints alongside mine and your presence via words from near and far are remembered with gratitude.

A special thank you to my dear friend Kaisa for the ongoing creative dialogue and collaborative space that saw this journal through from an idea to fruition.

Special thanks to my talented friends Germán and Peter for your sought-after photographic contributions.

Thank you to the wonderful staff at Balboa Press. From the first phone call, you shone the brightest light onto this collaborative effort. I am very grateful to you.

Wishing you well always,

Photography credits

Cover Photo—courtesy of Germán Limeres, smilesonthe camino.com

Pilgrim Shells – courtesy of Germán Limeres, smileonthe camino.com

Candles – Light of Hope - courtesy of Germán Limeres, smiles onthecamino.com

Kenzo – on the Way to Portamarin – courtesy of Germán Limeres, smilesonthecamino.com

The Rosary - courtesy Germán Limeres, smilesonthecamino.com

Follow the Arrow – courtesy of Germán Limeres, smilesonthe camino.com

At the Heart of Nature – courtesy of courtesy of Germán Limeres, smilesonthecamino.com

Finding the Way – courtesy of Germán Limeres, smilesonthe camino.com

El Camino, Back Cover —courtesy of Peter Campbell, petercambell.zenfolio.com.

Be an Angel along the Way, Devotion – Jesus I place my Trust in You, Love in the Simple Things in Life – are the Author's own work Tania Maree Herbert